THE P

CHRISSY WILLIAMS

SOARING PENGUIN PRESS
LONDON UK

THE JAM TRAP

CHRISSY WILLIAMS

All rights reserved. No part of this work covered by copyright hereon may be reproduced or used in any means - graphic, electronic, or mechanical, including copying, recording, taping, or information storage and retrieval systems - without written permission of the publisher.

Published by Soaring Penguin
4 Florence Terrace, London UK SW15 3RU
www.soaringpenguinpress.com

First published 2012
Third Edition printed 2013
© Copyright: Chrissy Williams
The moral right of the author has been asserted.
ISBN: 978 1 908030 03 0

Cover illustration by Lucian M. Stephenson

Printed and bound in the UK by PrintonDemand-Worldwide

*To Kieron
for the lunacy*

Wallet With The Charcoal

I thought I left your wallet with the charcoal. "Oh no," you said. Then I found it in my pocket. "But what was it doing in your pocket?" you asked in sombre tones. "I don't know," I said to you, patting my hand gently upon your head.

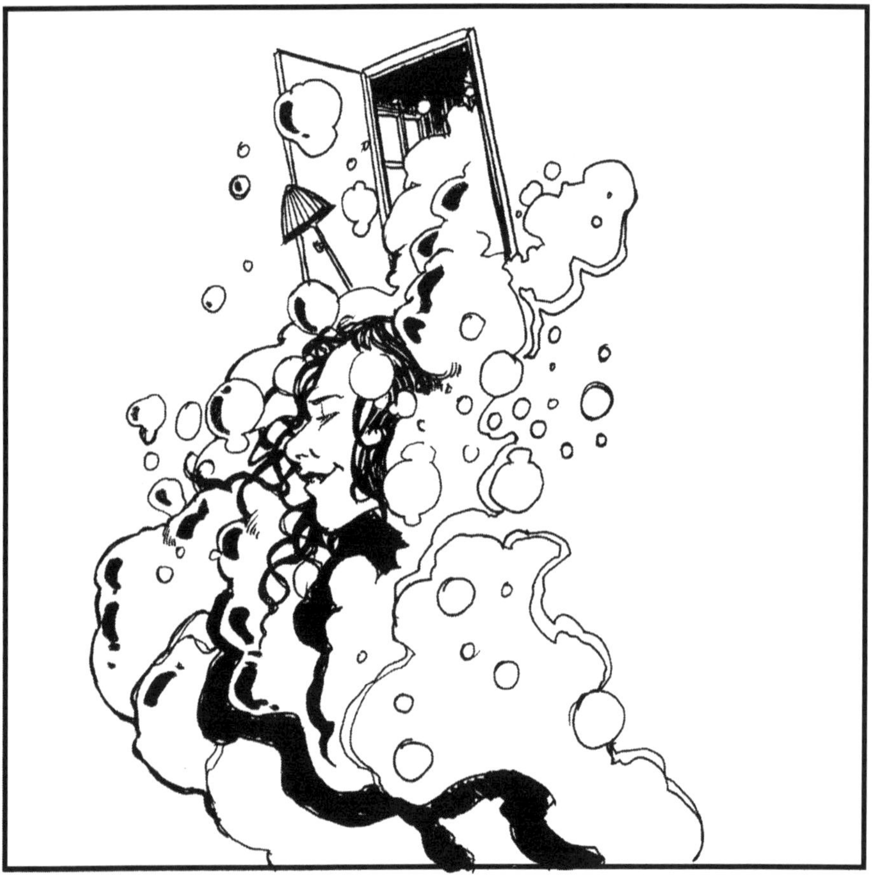

Bedroom Filled With Foam

"If you want to watch something in bed, I will come and watch something in bed with you. If you want to go straight to sleep, I may stay up a little longer as I'm not ready to go to sleep just yet. If, for some reason, we can't get into the bedroom, say, because the bedroom is filled with foam, not that I'm saying I have filled the bedroom with foam or anything, but if it was filled with foam, we could always watch something down here."

"Is it?"

"Is what?"

"Is the bedroom filled with foam?"

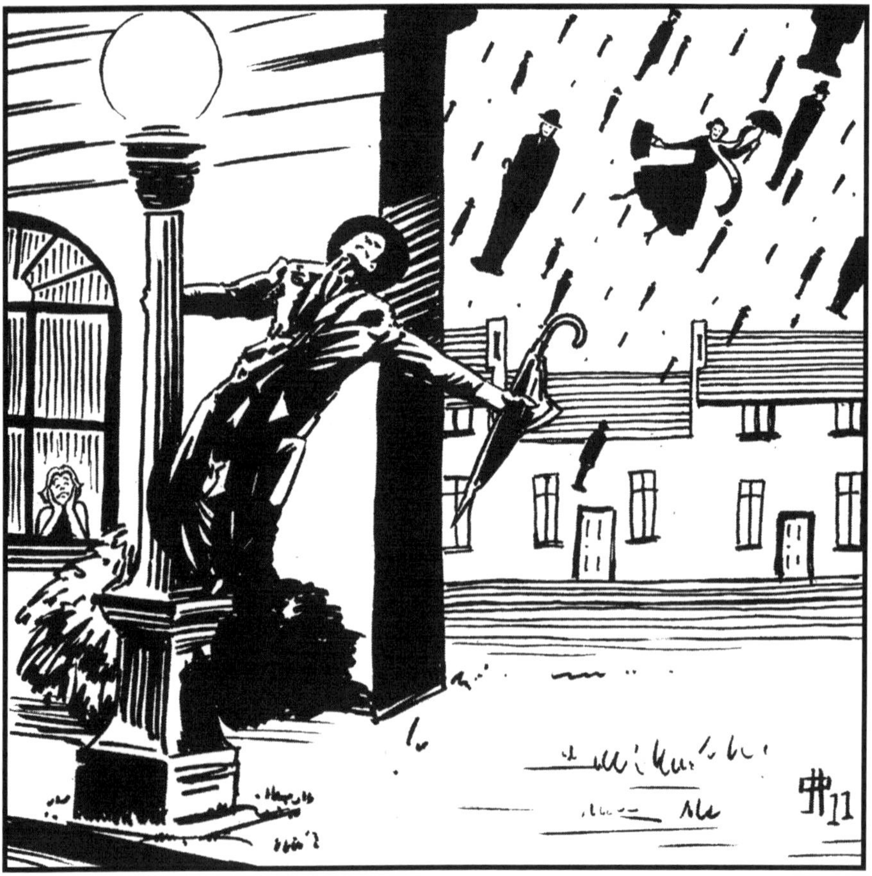

Wet Days Are The Worst

Wet days are the worst, when you find it impossible to shake me out of my most deeply-rooted beliefs, when I sit in the surplus bathroom, banging my head against the door, repeating over and over: "I believe the umbrella sellers are in league with the sky."

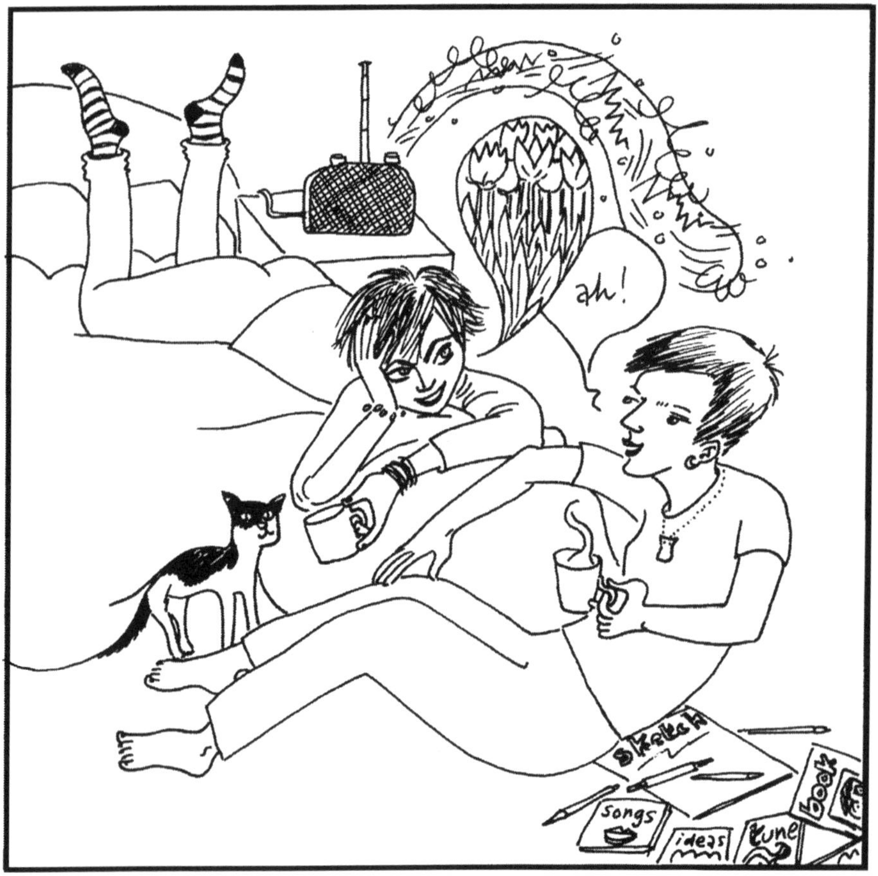
ah!
sketch
songs
ideas
tune
book

The ChewLips

"Do you like the ChewLips?" you asked.

"Yes, I do," I said.

"Do you like that song?" you asked.

"Which one?" I said.

"The one about time. We don't want to wait. No time. No time. We…"

"Oh yes, that one. Yes, I like that one," I said.

"Do you know what I don't like about the ChewLips?" you asked.

"What?" I said, turning to look at your eyebrows.

"I don't like the way their name said aloud sounds like 'tulips.'"

"ChewLips?" I asked incredulously.

"Tulips."

throat cleared!
WHEEZE
wrinkle!
?!
GRunt
cluck cluck
cluck cluck
*
RUSTLE!
whinny
splotch

"Hmmmmph…" You Said

"You realise we've communicated almost entirely in noises this evening?" I said.

"Hmmmmph…" you said.

"Words, words, words! Noise, noise, noise!" I said.

"Hmmmmph…" you said again, winking.

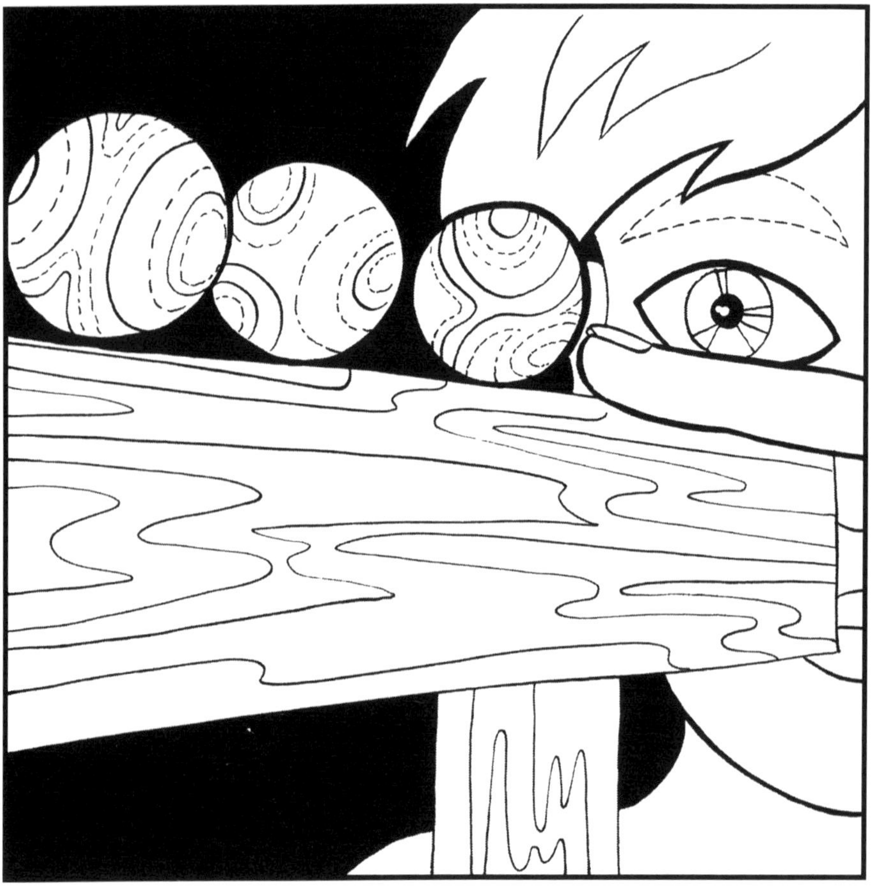

Three Marbles

"Hey, hey, hey," I said. "I've got three marbles in my DS case!"

"Hey!" you said, coming over, interested. "Those are my three marbles!"

"I know!" I said. "I took them from the box on the middle shelf in your brother's room!"

"Do you have any of your own?" you said to me, suddenly concerned.

"I have no use for marbles," I said, snapping the DS case shut.

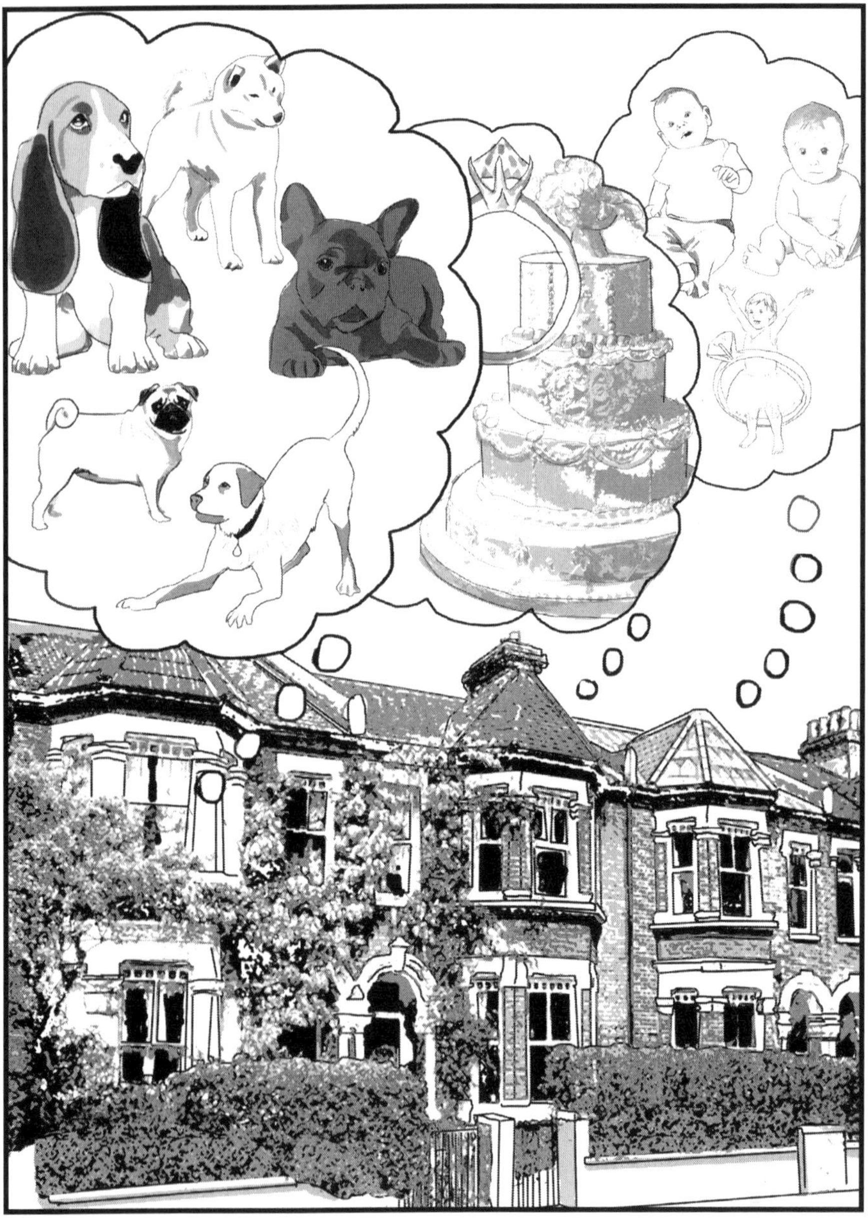

Clapham Is Where You Go

"What's Clapham like?" you asked. "Well," I said, rolling up my sleeves. "Clapham is where you go when you're ready to start having babies. And if you're not ready to start having babies before you move there, you will be after six months or thereabouts. Because everyone in Clapham is either a young undergraduate or someone who has moved there because they're ready to start having babies." "But we're not thinking about babies now," you said. "That's exactly right," I replied. "We're thinking about dogs."

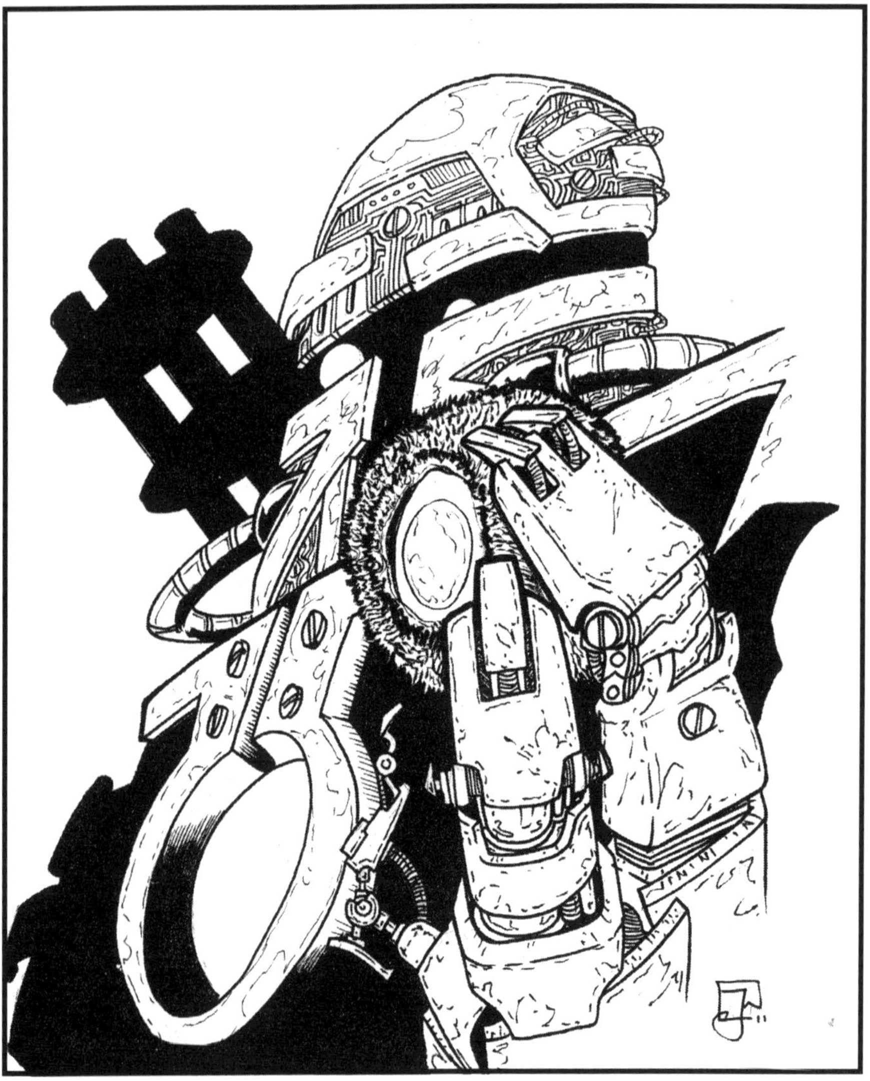

Integrated Killing Army Of Death-Humans

"What would you do if I was suddenly transported into a bleak future populated by a personalityless integrated killing army of death-humans and couldn't find a way to get back to you?" you asked.

"Weep," I said. "Then eat your scotch eggs."

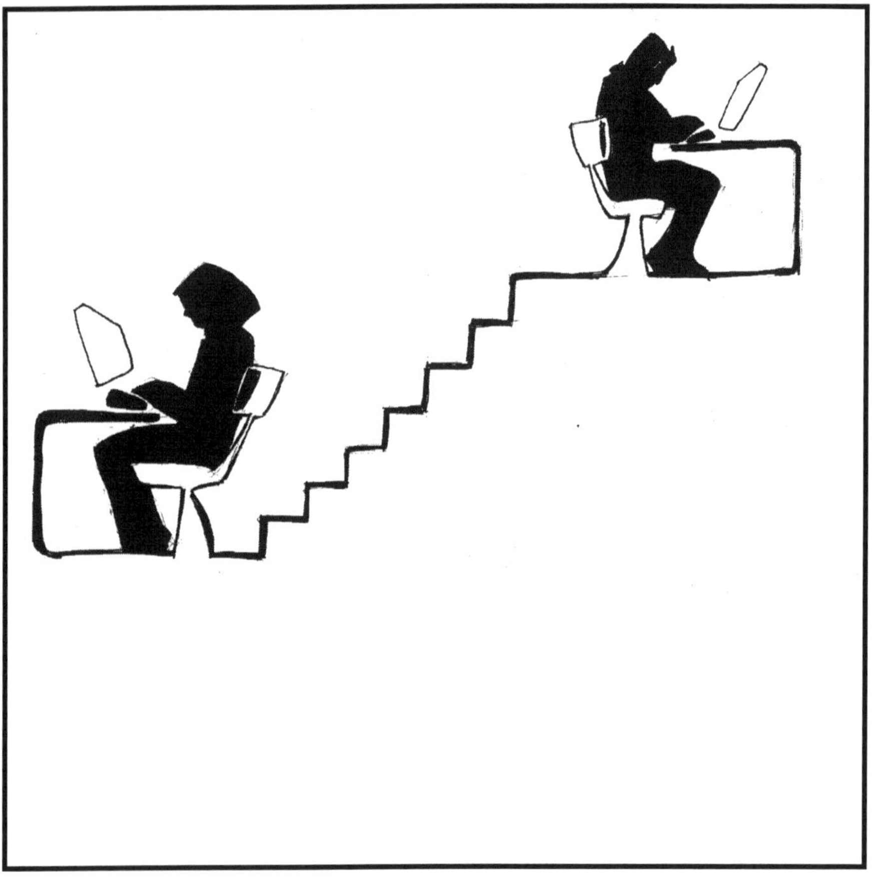

Talking To Each Other

"The cells in this spreadsheet aren't talking to each other," I called up the stairs from my desk by the door. "I think it's a problem with multiple pages linked in Excel that haven't translated to Googledocs properly. I don't want to manually relink everything. Is it okay if I email it?"

There was a pause.

Then you yelled down, "I think it's cute you said, 'talking to each other.'"

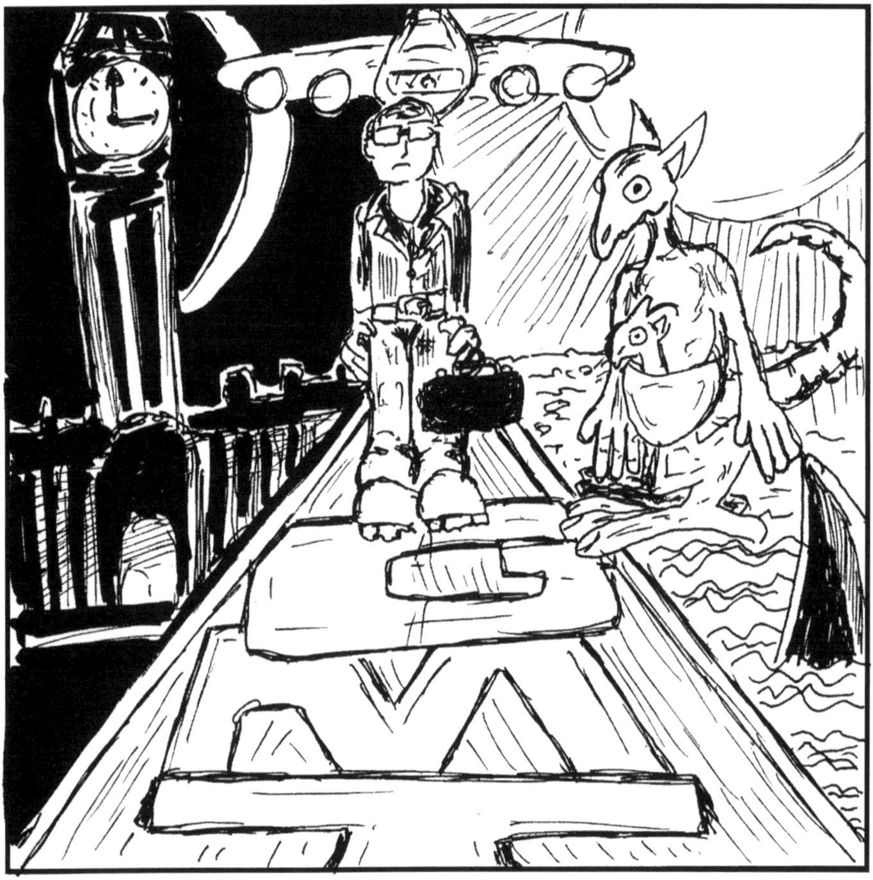

Is It Tomorrow?

"Is it tomorrow?" you asked with the jet lag.

"Yes," I replied. "It's tomorrow today."

"You're like some kind of time wizard," you said. "And I am Doctor Who. Only my time machine is my body, travelling forward very slowly."

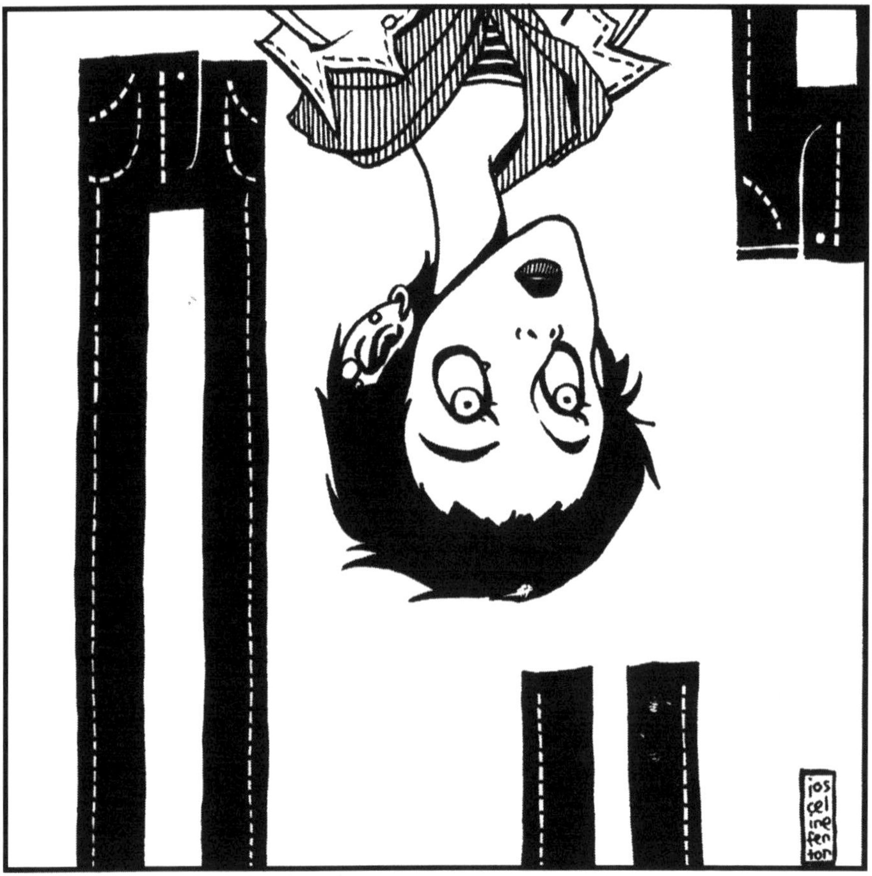
jos
cel
ine
fen
ton

Over Dave's Trousers

I knew you'd be out for ages, despite you saying you'd be home early because you were starting early, so I planned to be out for ages too only in a different part of town. I spilt some beer along the length of the table and into Dave's trousers and even though Dave was very nice about it, my guilt meant I remembered the very next thing he said to me with absolute clarity. He said:

"Everything is a test."

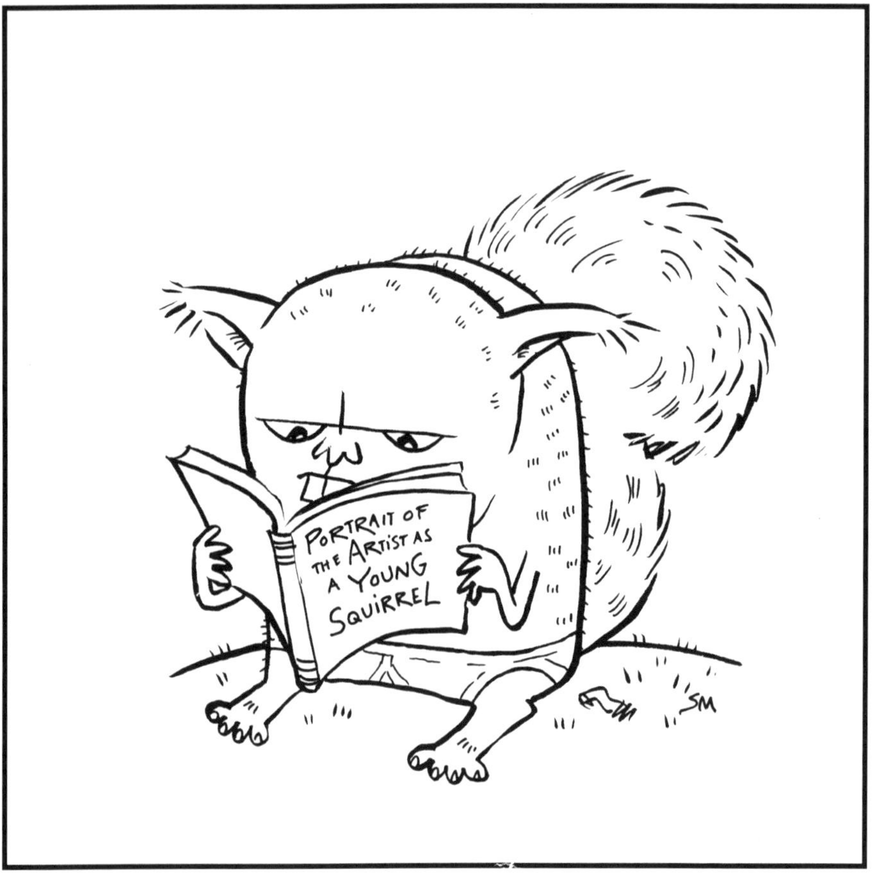
PORTRAIT OF THE ARTIST AS A YOUNG SQUIRREL
SM

Look, Look, Look

"Look, look, look," I said, gesturing frantically out of the 91 top deck window into someone's front garden. "There's a dog in that person's front garden that looks exactly like a squirrel!" "Mmm, yes, because of its tail," you said, feigning interest for a moment before going back to your book.

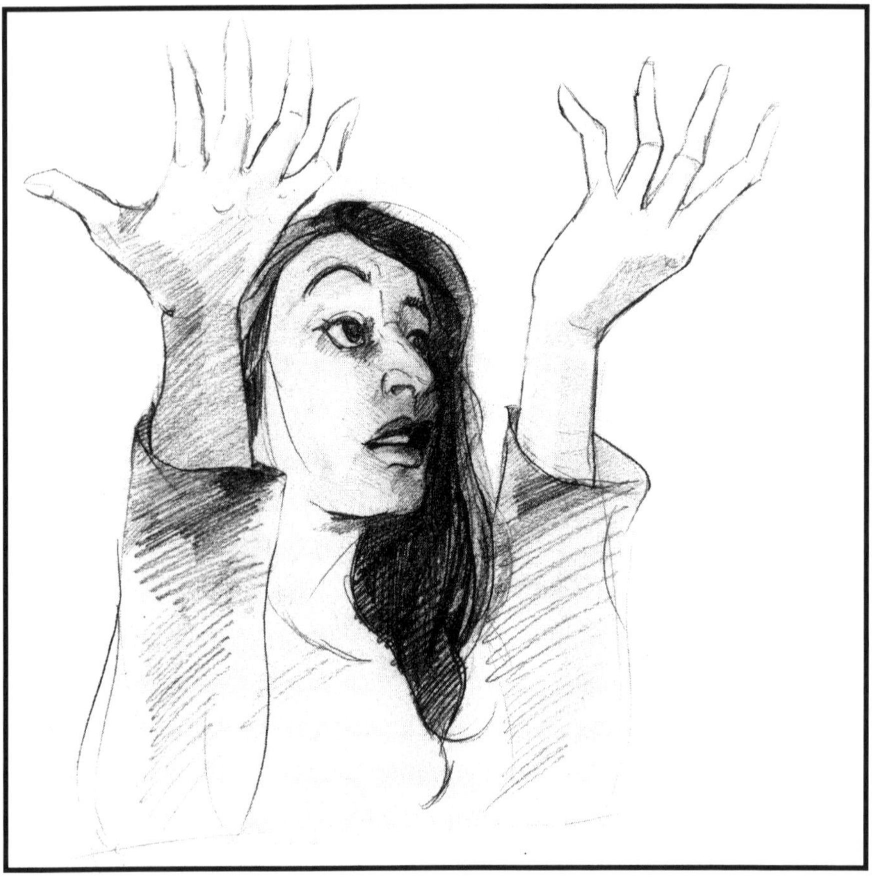

What Do You Think It Is?

"This thing doesn't have a plot," you observed.

"Nothing happens at all," you observed.

"It doesn't rhyme, at least not anywhere obvious," you observed.

"Just what the hell is it if there isn't a plot?" you asked.

"I don't know," I yelled, waving my arms around. "What do you think it is?"

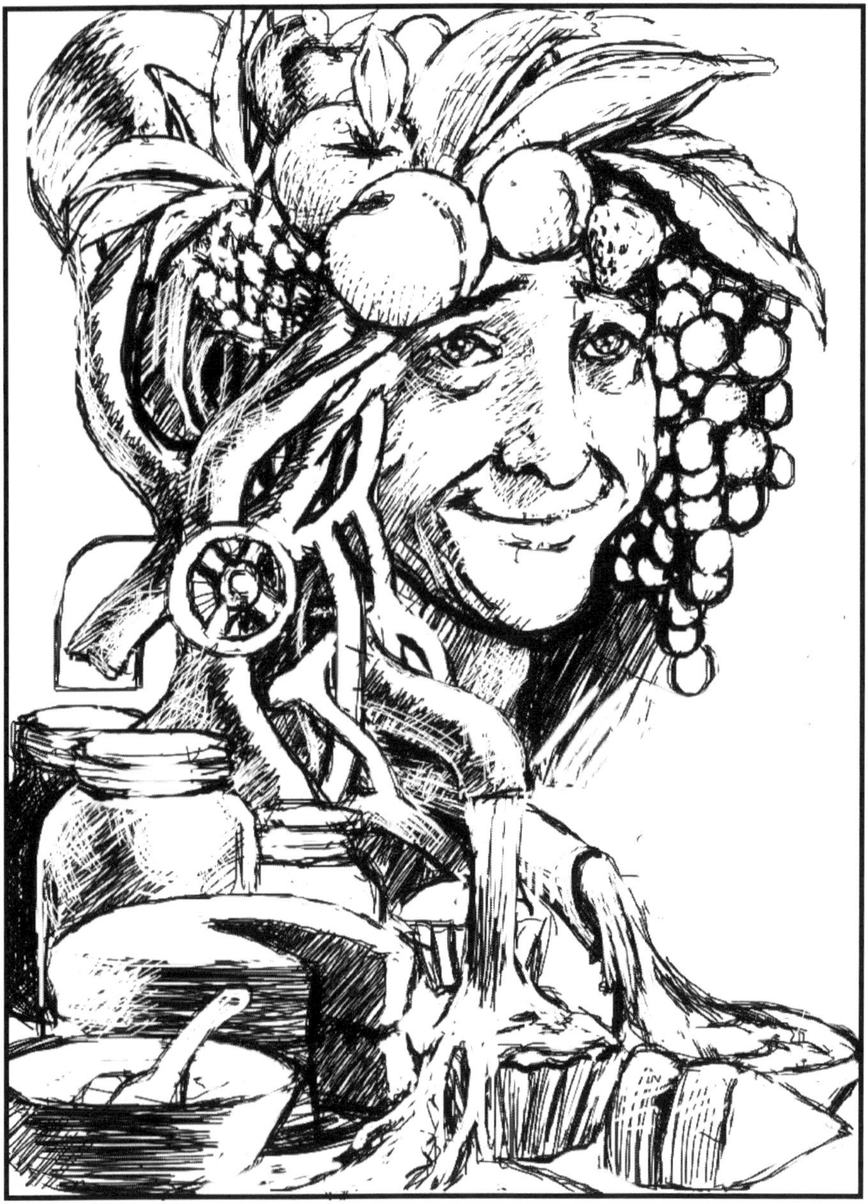

Jam Trap

"My body is structurally going the way of gravity," I said.

"Your brain will outlast your body, with luck," you said.

"My brain?" I said. "I think I have a brain like a jam trap."

"What does that mean?" you said.

I shrugged, beaming like an idiot.

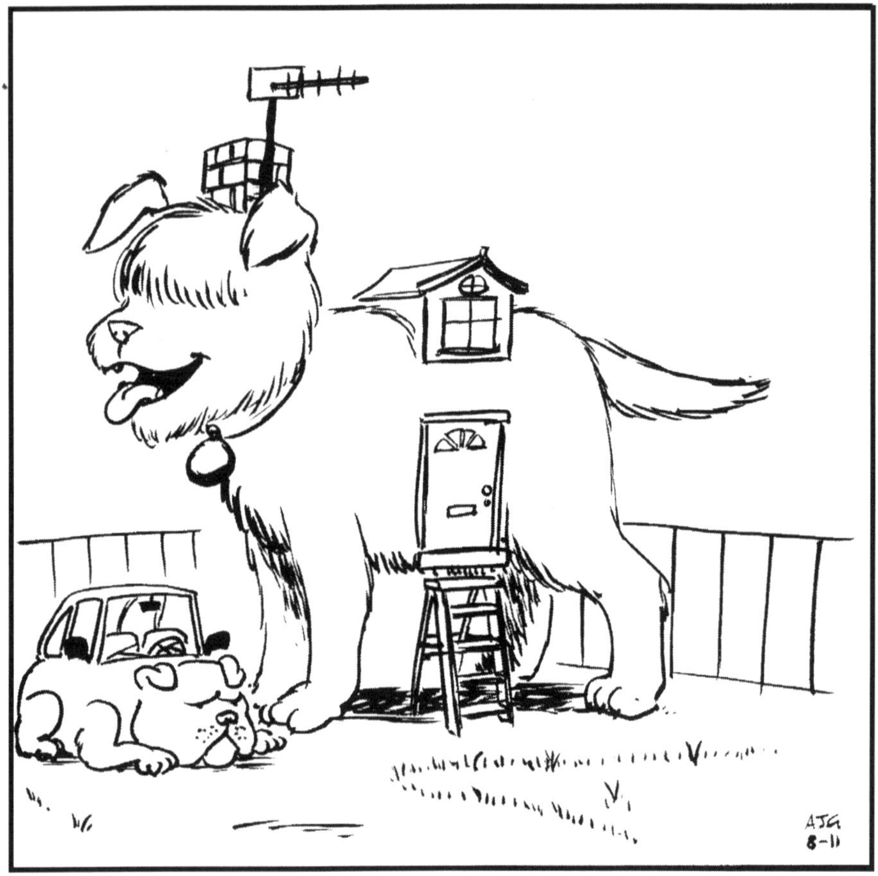
AJG
8-11

Ooh, Ooh, Ooh

"Ooh, ooh, ooh," I said, jabbing my finger at page 320 of the Encyclopedia of the Dog that was sat on my lap. "We could get a Bernese Mountain Dog!"

"We'd need to give it our bed to sleep in. We'd need to move out of the house."

"Then let's spend our money on an enormous dog we can hollow out and move into." I curled a bit closer into your shoulder, stroking the book while we slouched on the sofa.

"I don't think you've thought this through," you said.

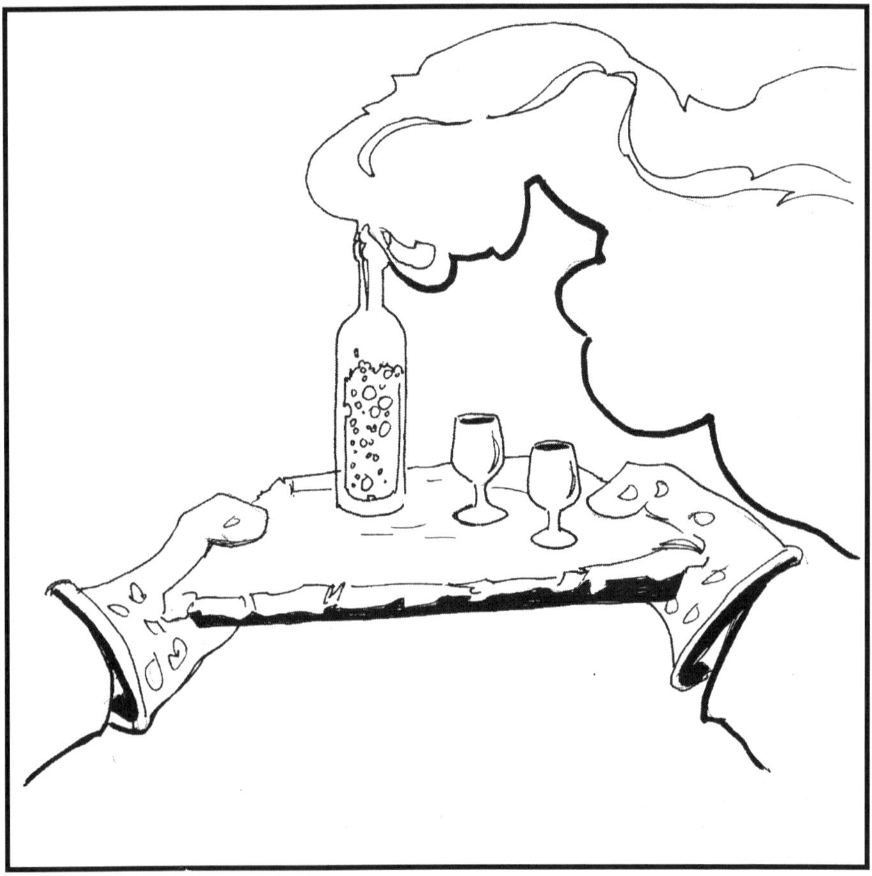

Where Have You Put The Wine?

"Where have you put the wine?"

"I've put the wine in the oven."

"You've put the wine in the oven?"

"I haven't put the wine in the oven."

"Where have you put the wine?"

"I've put the wine in the cold oven."

"You've put the wine in the fridge?"

"I've put the wine in the fridge."

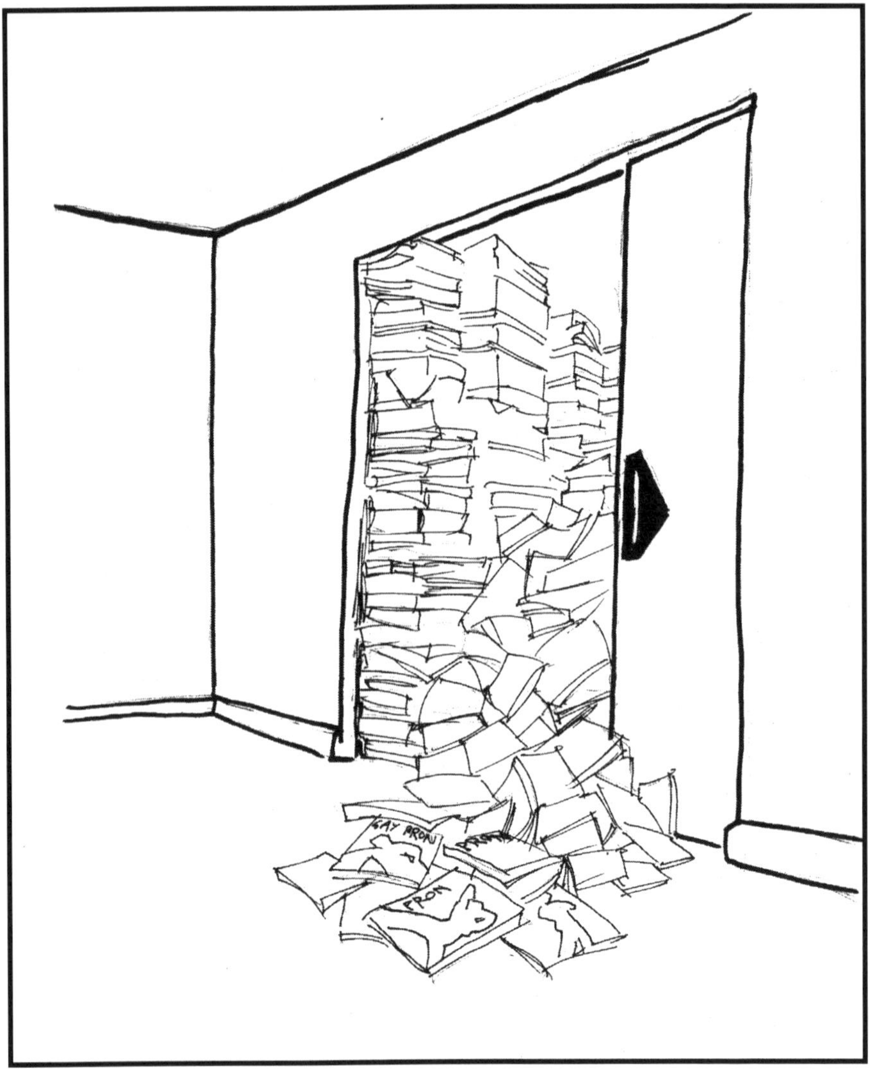
GAY PRON
PRON

Take Information Out Of One Room

I told you about the lecture and how furious I was at the notion that it is wrong to take information out of the one room in the whole world it is kept in and reproduce it faithfully and accurately in a place where anyone in the world can see it using an internet connection in their own room. "Why do some people persist in hating the internet?" I said in a loud, fast voice. "Well," you replied, "some people just hate free porn."

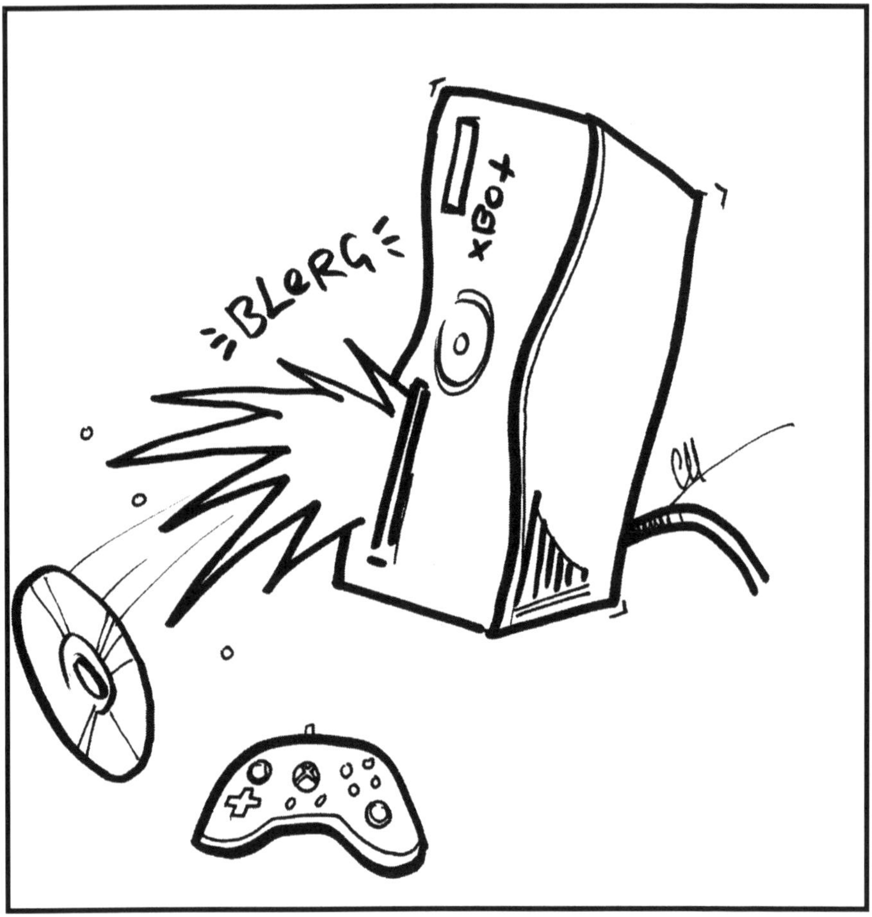
BLERG
XBOX

Confused, You Said

"The X-Box is confused," you said. "It won't play the DVD."

"Perhaps the wireless controller is confusing it?"

"Hmmmm… No… I don't think so..."

"Perhaps the Rock Band controller is confusing it?"

"Hmmmm… No… I don't think so..."

"Perhaps Francis Ford Coppola's interwoven dual narrative simultaneously sequelling and prequelling the original in an ambitious depiction of multiple generations of mafia history is confusing it?"

"Nope," you said with irritation, checking the tray. "You didn't put the disk in."

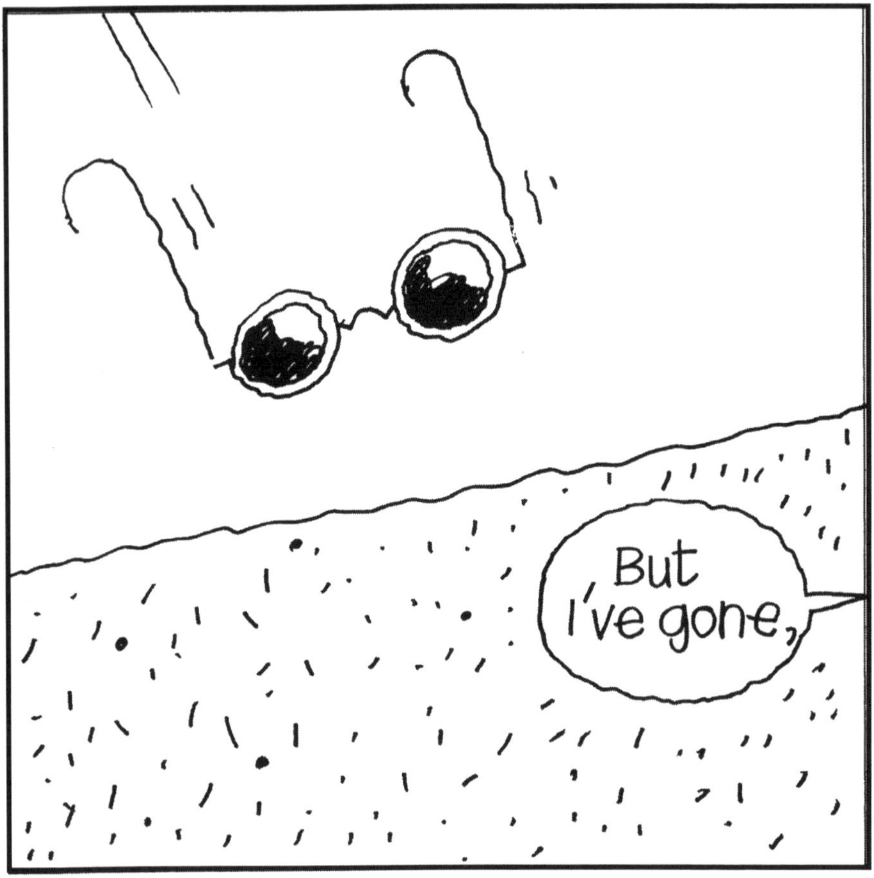
But I've gone,

Why Are Your Glasses Still On?

"Why is the light still on?" you asked with your eyes closed. "Why are your glasses still on?" I asked with my eyes open. "Touché," you said, "okay, here's the plan: on the count of three, you go for the light and I'll ditch my glasses, then we'll meet back here in two seconds. Three. Two. One." "Aha!" I said, two seconds later. "I made it back before you. That means I won." "But I've gone," you answered. "I am staying away. It was purely a ruse to escape you."

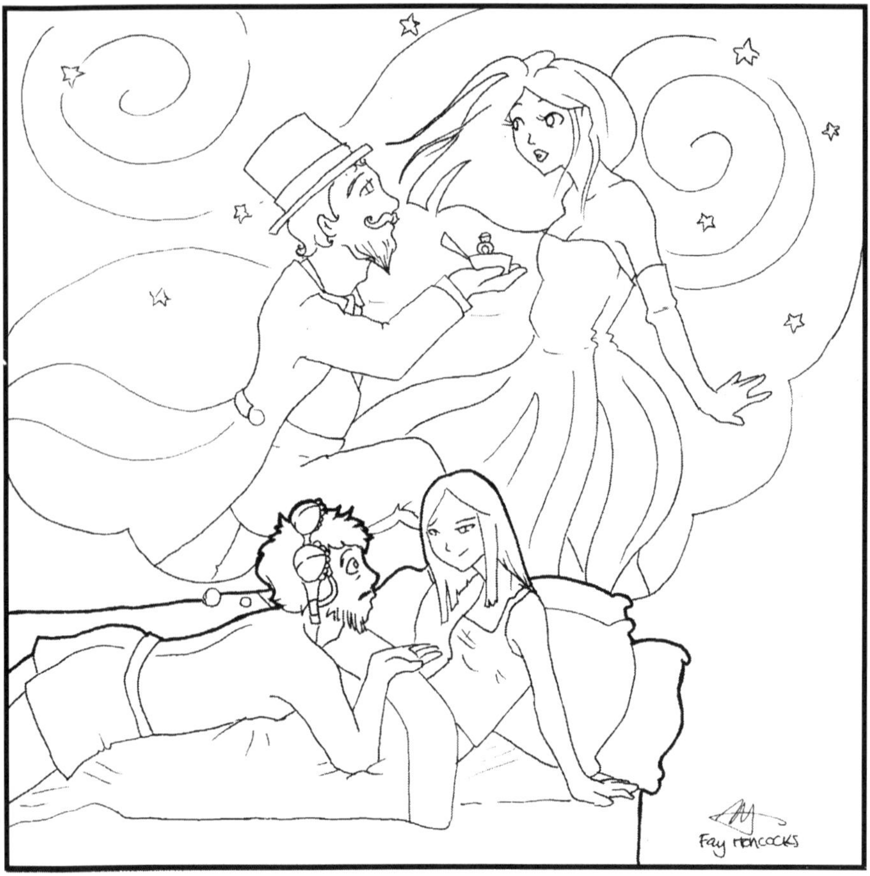
Fay HANCOCKS

Will You Marry Me?

"Will you marry me?" you said in bed, drunk, after a long night out.

"What?" I said, also drunk.

"Will you marry me?" you said, throwing yourself over in the duvet dark to face me.

"What?" I said again.

"Will you marry me?" you said, far more deliberately than the first two times so I'd know you were being serious.

"Well," I said, "I think your sense of timing is inappropriate."

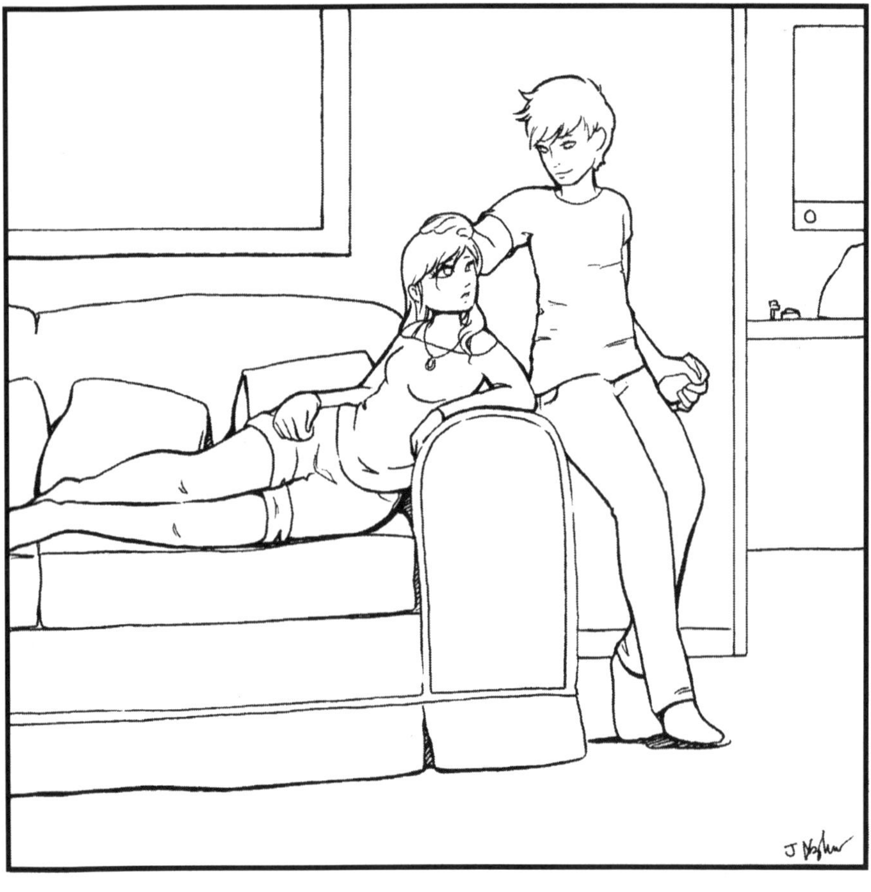

Four Hours Away

I was telling you about visiting my cousins in Italy and how they took me up into the mountains north of Turin where I used to go as a girl and how far away it seems from everything and how my one cousin was telling me about bears that used to roam there while my other cousin was telling me about a trip they did up to one of the mountain lakes that took four hours to walk to and then I agreed with you when you said: "I can't remember the last time I was four hours away from anything."

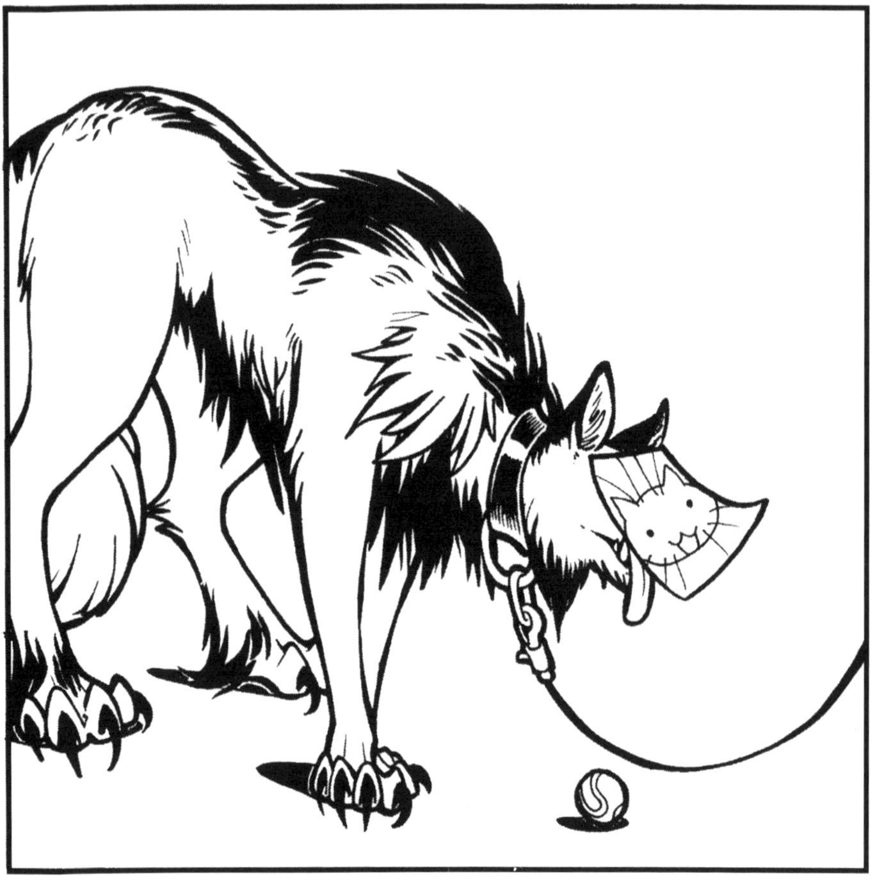

I'm Not Falling For That

"Maybe we should get a cat?"

"Cat?"

"A cat we could buy a collar for."

"Collar?"

"A cat we could put on a lead and take for walks."

"Lead?"

"A cat we could call Rex and teach tricks to."

"And where, exactly, would we get such a cat?"

"From Battersea Dogs Home!"

"I'm not falling for that."

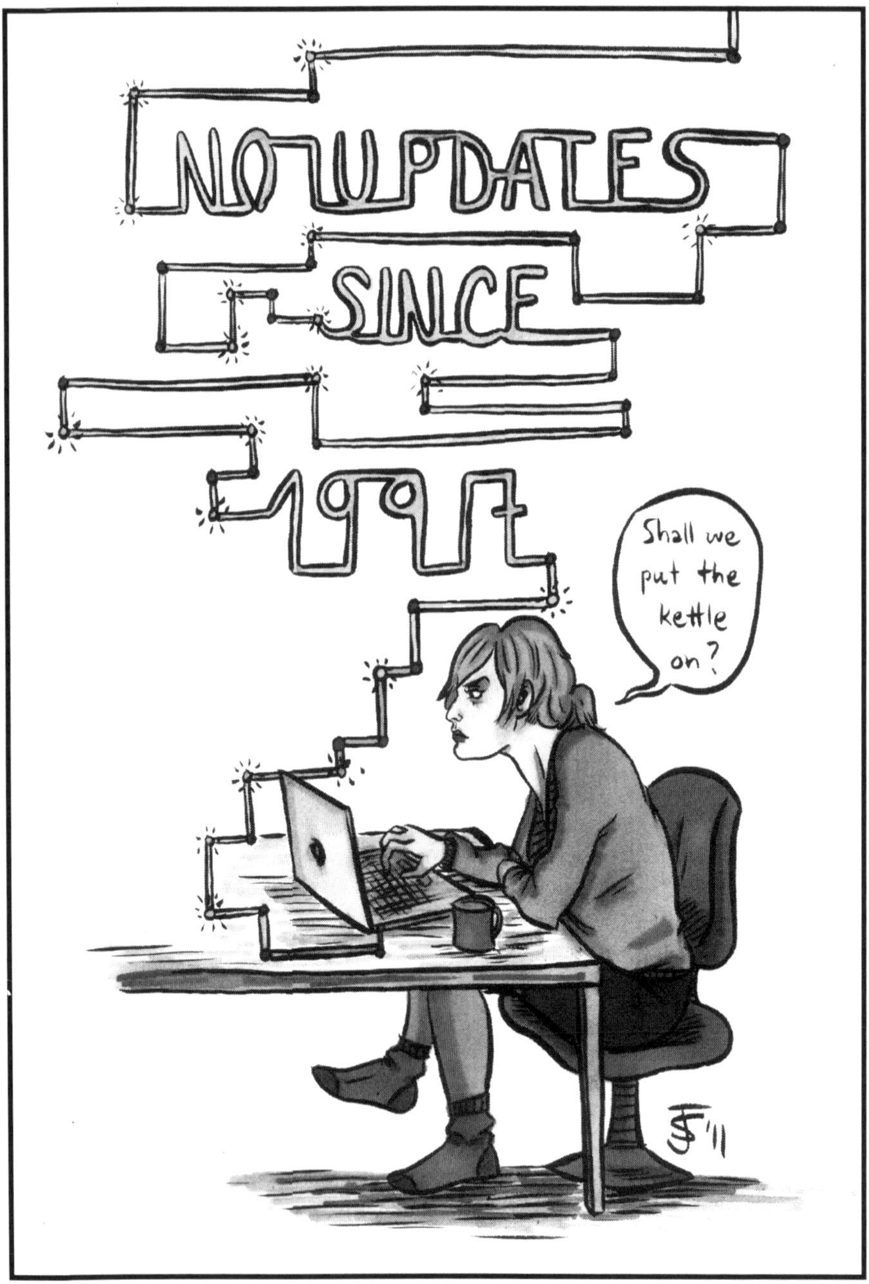

NO UPDATES SINCE 1997
Shall we put the kettle on?

Digital Ghost Towns

I forwarded you the thing about the British Library's web archiving project and you said it looked very interesting and I suddenly remembered that time I was trying to google some old poetry sites and kept seeing things like No Updates Since 1997 and how depressing it was and how somehow it was even more depressing seeing these digital ghost towns than it was for a physical magazine to simply stop making any new issues and then how the more I looked the more I realised the internet is full of dead ends and holes and the bits of it that actually work are just bright lights shining in a desert, not like Vegas because Vegas is off-putting to lots of people so it's a bad analogy but I just mean that when the lights are working they're wonderful and anything abandoned especially something creative makes me sad but it's part of the process I suppose and we just have to try and avoid these holes and my god how many blogs will there even be online in 50 years' time and have we got another 2000 years of blogging coming up and shouldn't we be setting up grander projects that will last brightly forever without getting lost on the internet and just what are we playing at anyway?

"Shall we put the kettle on?" is what I say.

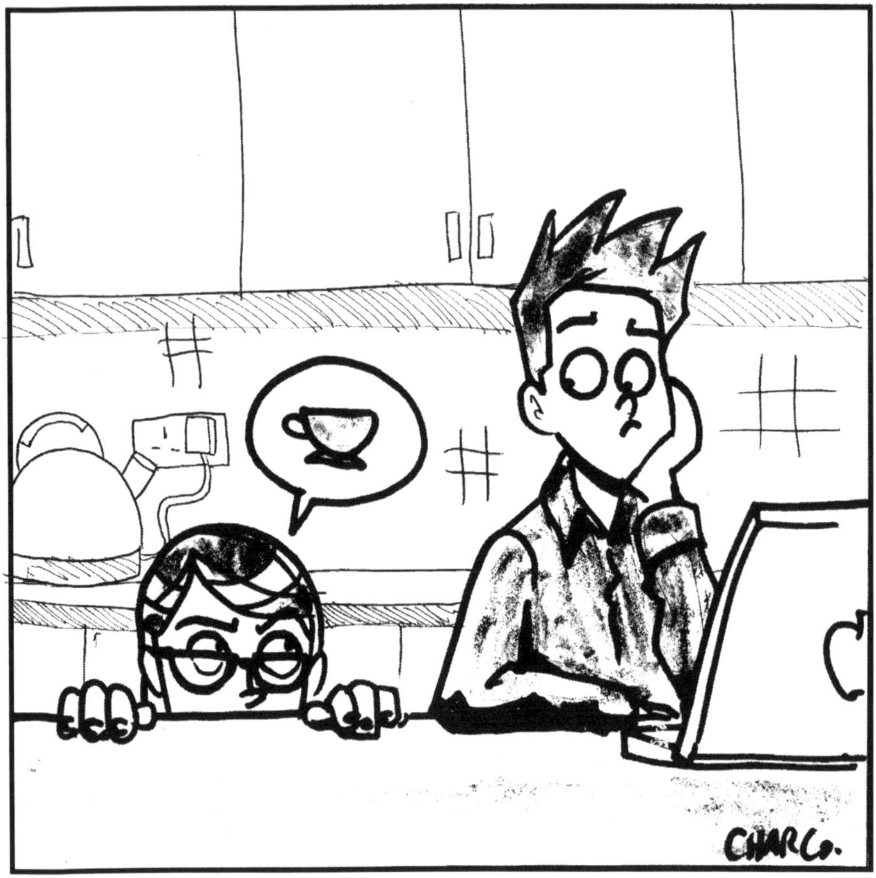
CHARCo.

Tea Is Our Solution To Everything

"Do you want a tea?" you asked.

"Why not?" I replied.

"Do you know why this is going to be the best cup of tea in the world?" you asked.

"Tell me why," I replied.

"Because not only is it being made and served in our very own kitchen," you said, "but because we have chocolate-covered hobnobs in the cupboard, and I'm not afraid to use them."

Acknowledgements

With thanks to the lovely folk at Silkworms Ink who originally published some of these poems.

http://www.silkwormsink.com

The Poet

Chrissy Williams lives in London and has had work published in various magazines including *The Rialto, Horizon Review, Anon, Under The Radar, Fuselit, Rising* and *Southbank Poetry*. Her work has also appeared in Salt's *Best British Poetry 2011* anthology, in the *Oxfam Book of Young Poets, Stop/Sharpening/Your/Knives* and in anthologies published by Sidekick Books. She is also Joint Editor of *Poetry Digest*, the world's finest edible poetry journal. She has an MA in Modern and Contemporary Poetry from Bristol University and is the coordinator for the Saison Poetry Library's magazine digitisation project at www.poetrymagazines.org.uk.

Chrissy's blog may be found at www.chrissywilliams.blogspot.com

The Artists

Lizz Lunney (lizz@lizzlizz.com; http://www.lizzlizz.com) illustrated *Wallet With The Charcoal*

John Aggs illustrated *Bedroom Filled with Foam*

Paul Rafferty (http://www.psrafferty.deviantart.com) illustrated *Wet Days Are The Worst*

Jeremy Day (http://www.jeremyday.org.uk) illustrated *The ChewLips*

Ellen Lindner (http://www.littlewhitebird.com) illustrated *"Hmmmmph..." You Said*

Ellen Lindner also illustrated *Three Marbles*

Laurenn McCubbin (laurennmcc@gmail.com; http://www.laurennmccubbin.dreamhosters.com) illustrated *Clapham Is Where You Go*

Joe Ward (thesloarth@hotmail.com; http://captainsnikt.tumblr.com) illustrated *Integrated Killing Army of Death-Humans*

John Maybury (john@spacebabe113.co.uk; http://www.spacebabe113.co.uk) illustrated *Talking To Each Other*

Christopher A Geary (http://www.gearysworld.blogspot.com) illustrated *Is It Tomorrow?*

Josceline Fenton (http://www.mildtarantula.com) illustrated *Over Dave's Trousers*

Sarah McIntyre (http://www.jabberworks.co.uk) illustrated *Look, Look, Look*

Sarah Gordon (sarah@ratherlemony.com; http://ratherlemony.com) illustrated *What Do You Think It Is?*

Meirion Jones (meirion@bardsofnemeton.co.uk; http://www.bardsofnemeton.co.uk) illustrated *Jam Trap*

Arthur Goodman (http://www.favouritecrayon.co.uk) illustrated *Ooh, Ooh, Ooh*

John Maybury also illustrated *Where Have You Put The Wine?*

John Maybury also illustrated *Take Information Out Of One Room*

Caspar Wijngaard (caspart8@yahoo.com) illustrated *Confused, You Said*

Sally Kindberg (http://www.sallykindberg.co.uk) illustrated *Why Are Your Glasses Still On?*

Fay Hancocks (http://www.parfay.co.uk) illustrated *Will You Marry Me?*

Jodie Azhar (http://tangentine.com) illustrated *Four Hours Away*

Lucian M. Stephenson (http://www.mrlucian.com) illustrated *I'm Not Falling For That*

Julia Scheele (julia.scheele@gmail.com; http://idontlikemyhairneat.tumblr.com) illustrated *Digital Ghost Towns*

Ciaran Lucas (http://www.ciaranlucas.com) illustrated *Tea Is Out Solution To Everything*